CAT NAPS

CAT NAPS

RONNIE
SELLERS
PRODUCTIONS
-Gift Books-
PORTLAND, MAINE

Life is hard,
then you nap.

Anonymous

The idea of calm
exists in a sitting cat.

Jules Renard

There is more to life
than increasing its speed.

Mohandas Gandhi

If I didn't woke up,
I'd still be sleeping!

Yogi Berra

I don't know why it is we are in such a hurry to get up when we fall down. You might think we would lie there and rest a while.

Max Forrester Eastman

If there were to be
a universal sound
depicting peace,
I would surely vote
for the purr.

Barbara L. Diamond

The best cure
for insomnia is
to get a lot of sleep.

W.C. Fields

Light be the earth upon you, lightly rest.

Euripides

Learning to ignore
things is one of the
great paths to
inner peace.

Robert J. Sawyer

How beautiful it is to do nothing,
and then to rest afterward.

Spanish proverb

Champagne wishes
and caviar dreams . . .

Anonymous

Cats are rather delicate creatures
and they are subject to a good many
ailments, but I never heard of one
who suffered from insomnia.

Joseph Wood Crutch

A cat pours his
body on the
floor like water.
It is restful just
to see him.

William Lyon Phelps

I have never taken
any exercise except
sleeping and resting.

Mark Twain (Samuel L. Clemens)

Who among us hasn't envied a cat's ability to ignore the cares of daily life and to relax completely?

Karen Brademeyer

Take rest;
a field that has rested
gives a bountiful crop.

Ovid

The secret of happiness
is to make others believe
they are the cause of it.

Al Batt

Oh sleep! It is a gentle thing,
Beloved from pole to pole.

Samuel Taylor Coleridge

Slow down and enjoy life.
It's not only the scenery
you miss by going too fast
– you also miss the sense
of where you are going
and why.

Eddie Cantor

Sleep is the
best meditation.

Tenzin Gyatso,
the 14th Dalai Lama

There's never enough
time to do all the
nothing you want.

Bill Watterson,
"Calvin and Hobbes"

Loafing needs no explanation
and is its own excuse.

Christopher Morley

Yawn and the world
yawns with you.
Snore and you
sleep alone.

Anonymous

Nature does not
hurry, yet everything
is accomplished.

Lao Tzu

There is more refreshment and stimulation in a nap, even of the briefest, than in all the alcohol ever distilled.

Edward Lucas

No day is so bad it can't
be fixed with a nap.

Carrie Snow

Dreams are only thoughts you didn't
have time to think about during the day.

Author unknown

Very little is needed
to make a happy life.

Marcus Aurelius Antoninus

Taking a nap,
feet planted
against a cool wall.

Matsuo Basho, "Taking a Nap"

If there is one spot
of sun spilling onto
the floor, a cat will
find it and soak it up.

Jean Asper-McIntosh

It takes a lot of time
to be a genius, you
have to sit around so
much doing nothing,
really doing nothing.

Gertrude Stein

Slow down and everything you are chasing

will come around and catch you.

John DePaola

The fog comes
on little cat feet.

Carl Sandberg, "The Fog"

Subliminal kitty messages?
"You are getting very sleepy"
is not a command when said
to a cat; it is an eternal truth.

Ari Ripkin

Follow your bliss and doors will open where there were no doors before.

Joseph Campbell

Kittens are born with their eyes shut. They open them in about six days, take a look around, then close them again for the better part of their lives.

Stephen Baker

The time to relax is when you don't have time for it.

Author unknown

BINOCULARS

A FIELD GUIDE TO THE BUTTERFLIES OF
The East

BIRDS

. . . there is a luxury in being

quiet in the heart of chaos.

Virginia Woolf

Everything I know
I learned from my cat:
When you're hungry, eat.
When you're tired,
nap in a sunbeam.
When you go to the vet's,
pee on your owner.

Gary Smith

There is no need to go to India or anywhere else to find peace. You will find that deep place of silence right in your room, your garden, or even your bathtub.

Dr. Elisabeth Kübler Ross, M.D.

A little drowsing cat is an image of perfect beatitude.

Jules Champfleury

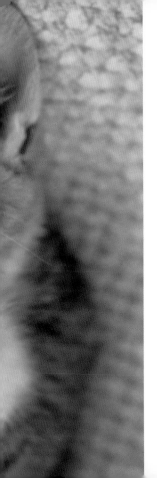

Don't underestimate
the value of doing nothing,
of just going along, listening
to all the things you can't hear,
and not bothering.

"Pooh's Little Instruction Book"

To sleep is
an act of faith.

Barbara G. Harrison

He seems the incarnation of everything soft and silky and velvety, without a sharp edge in his composition, a dreamer whose philosophy is sleep and let sleep.

Saki (H.H. Munro)

Now I see the secret of
the making of the best
persons. It is to grow in
the open air and to eat
and sleep with the earth.

Walt Whitman,
"Song of the Open Road"

It takes a lot of courage
to show your dreams
to someone else.

Erma Bombeck

Festinalente:

Make haste slowly.

Prowling his own quiet backyard or asleep by the fire, he is still only a whisker away from the wilds.

Jean Burden

The future belongs to those who believe
in the beauty of their dreams.

Eleanor Roosevelt

Rest is not idleness,
and to lie sometimes
on the grass under a tree
on a summer's day,
listening to the murmur
of the water, or watching
the clouds float across
the sky, is by no means
a waste of time.

J. Lubbock

Which is more beautiful:
feline movement
or feline stillness?

Elizabeth Hamilton

A good laugh and
a long sleep are
the best cures in
the doctor's book.

Irish proverb

Cats are connoisseurs
of comfort.

James Herriot

Credits

photo © Torahiko Yamashita/Photonica; pp. 88-89 photo © PhotoAlto/Creatas; pp. 90-91 photo © Neo Vision/ Photonica; pp. 92-93 photo © Koichiro Shimauchi/ Photonica; pp. 94-95 photo © Torahiko Yamashita/ Photonica; pp. 96-97 photo © Torahiko Yamashita/Photonica; pp. 98-99 photo © Grace Davies; pp. 100-101 photo © Torahiko Yamashita/Photonica; pp. 102-103 photo © Koichiro Shimauchi/Photonica; pp. 104-105 photo © Torahiko Yamashita/Photonica; pp. 106-107 photo © Torahiko Yamashita/Photonica; pp. 108-109 photo © Koichiro Shimauchi/Photonica.

Published by Ronnie Sellers Productions, Inc.

P.O. Box 818, Portland, Maine 04104
For ordering information:
Phone: 1-800-MAKE-FUN (800-625-3386)
Fax: (207) 772-6814
Visit our Web site: www.makefun.com
E-mail: rsp@rsvp.com

Series Editor: Robin Haywood
Photo Editor: Amanda Mooney
Designer: Patti Urban

ISBN: 1-56906-519-5

Second Printing

Printed in China